This book belongs to . . .  Todd

Captain Kangaroo's
Whole World
Catalog

Compiled by Jim Krayer
Illustrated by Judith Hoffman Corwin
Platt & Munk, Publishers/New York

Library of Congress Card Catalog No: 75— 24622
ISBN: 0— 8228— 8980— 3

QUESTOR®
A QUESTOR COMPANY

A Message From Captain Kangaroo

To the grown-up who now holds this book:
If you are a parent, or relative, or friend of the child who owns this book, these introductory words are meant for you.

Between the covers of this Captain Kangaroo Whole World Catalogue there is, indeed, a world of fun and information. But if your special child is very young, he will need help in exploring that world. This book has been carefully designed to bring child and parent together in a mutually rewarding adventure of shared experience.

There are many activities and projects that the child will enjoy alone; but other features . . . read-aloud stories, games, playtimes . . . are meant to be shared by adult and child. Then there are group activities for parties or rainy days that require a degree of adult supervision. In many cases I hope that you will help the child to get started on projects and then let his imagination and creativity have free rein. What wonderfully exciting and unexpected treasures are revealed in this way!

So, please, *do* get involved with this book. I am sure the experience will be warm and entertaining and— best of all—one that will bring you and that very special young person even closer to each other.

Affectionately,

Captain Kangaroo

CARTON TRAIN

This is something you can make when your friends come to play at your place.

You'll need at least one big cardboard carton for each person in the train. Remove or push up the bottoms.

On both sides of the first carton draw big locomotive wheels. Take an empty delicatessen container (or make a cylinder from construction paper) and tape it to the front for a headlight. Underneath, draw a cow catcher. Take a paper towel tube and tape it to the inside of the front part of the carton for the smokestack. There you have your engine.

towel tube

deli container or paper headlight

Draw different railroad cars on the other cartons.

You can have a coal car—

—or a passenger car—

—or a boxcar—

—or a circus car—

—or a caboose—

—towel tube for stove pipe.

Remember to draw on both sides of the boxes. Use bright colors to make your train look happy.

When you've finished, each person steps into a box, pulls it up around his waist, and gets in line. Now you're a train! Don't forget—the engine goes first and the caboose comes along last. Take turns being engineer, conductor, and brakeman.

You can make a smaller, pull-toy train by decorating several shoeboxes to look like an engine and cars, and tying them together with string.

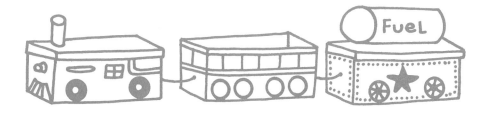

If you can find an empty salt or oatmeal box, you can tape it to a shoebox top to make a tank car.

Here are some songs to sing on your train trips.

There are not many steam trains left today. But years ago they were the pride of the railroads. This is what some of the engines looked like.

Down By The Station

Down by the station
Early in the morning,
See the little Puffer Billies
All in a row.
See the station master
Pull a little handle—
Puff, puff—choo, choo—
Off we go.

(This can be sung as a round)

Workin' on the Railroad

Verse I've been workin' on the railroad
All the live-long day.
I've been workin' on the railroad
Just to pass the time away.

Can't you hear the whistle blowin',
"Rise up so early in the morn"?
Can't you hear the Captain callin',
"Dinah, blow your horn"?

Chorus Dinah won't you blow,
Dinah won't you blow,
Dinah won't you blow your horn?
      (Repeat)

Someone's in the kitchen with Dinah,
Someone's in the kitchen I know.
Someone's in the kitchen with Dinah,
Strummin' on the old banjo.

Fee, fie, fiddle-dee-ei-oh
Fee, fie, fiddle-dee-ei-oh-oh-oh-oh.
Fee, fie, fiddle-dee-ei-oh
Strummin' on the old banjo.

When you go to the library, ask for a book about the wonderful trains of the past.

Dot·to·Dot
Follow the dots in order.

MAKING MUSIC

Let's make music!

Did you know that there are many musical instruments that you can make using ordinary objects that you can find around the house. Rhythm instruments are the easiest to make and play—and probably the most fun.

With just a few simple objects, you and your friends can have a whole rhythm band.

Bongo drums

Empty, two-pound coffee cans with plastic lids make very fine drums. Use the eraser end of an unsharpened pencil for the beater—or ask an older person to force the pointed end of a stick into a small rubber ball—the kind you use to play jacks.

If you want your drum to look fancier, you can make designs on construction paper and tape it around the can.

If you can find an empty one-pound coffee can, you can have a drum that makes a higher sound—and you can even tape two or three different sizes together to make bongo drums.

Maracas

Maracas are rattle-like instruments that you shake to make music. Real maracas look like this but you can make your own from empty cans or plastic food containers.

Empty frozen orange juice cans are a good size. Wash them well, put a handful of uncooked rice or dried beans in each can, then tape on the lids tightly and shake to make music.

Of course, you can decorate these, too, if you like.

Plastic food containers are good, too. They make the best sound when held sideways and shaken up and down.

Try different amounts of rice or beans until you get the sound you want. Don't forget to tape on the lids—or you'll have rice all over the floor!

Claves

Claves (pronounced "klahvays") are just two pieces of wood, struck together to make musical sounds. You can make your own with a wooden ruler and an unsharpened pencil.

The most important thing is to cup your left hand (right hand, if you're left handed) like this, then lay the ruler across the heel of your hand and your knuckles so that there is a space underneath. This will give you the proper sound when you hit the ruler with the pencil to make music.

Try different positions of the ruler until you get the best high, bright tone. If you hold the ruler in the palm of your hand and hit it with the pencil, you will hear how dull and unmusical the sound is.

Scrapers

Scrapers are easy, too. Just take two pieces of scrap wood and have someone tack rough sandpaper around them. When you rub the blocks together, the paper makes a rhythmic scraping sound.

Castanets

Castanets are Spanish rhythm instruments that are held in the palm of the hand and clicked with the fingers. Usually in Spain they are played by a dancer while he or she does one of many folk dances that the Spanish love.

You can make your own button castanets. Ask Mother for 4 big buttons—the larger, the better. Take 4 heavy duty rubber bands and cut each one to make a straight length of rubber.

Using a toothpick to help you, push the two ends of each rubber band through opposite holes in each button. Do this from the front of the button.

Pull the ends of the bands as far as they will go and then tie a knot in each one to make a loop just big enough to fit around your finger.

Now slip your castanets onto the middle finger and thumb of each hand, and click away! Try dancing as you play.

Here are some good songs to sing and play with your rhythm band

MARCHING SONGS

(In these songs, the basic rhythm is: *One*-two, *ONE*-two.)

Yankee Doodle.

Yankee Doodle went to town
Riding on a pony,
Stuck a feather in his hat
And called it macaroni.
    Yankee Doodle keep it up,
    Yankee Doodle Dandy.
    Mind the music and the step
    And with the girls be handy.

This Old Man

1. This old man
   He played one,
   He played Nick Nack on my drum,
   With a Nick Nack Paddy Whack give a dog a bone,
   This old man came rolling home.

2. This old man
   He played two,
   He played Nick Nack on my shoe, etc.

3. This old man
   He played three,
   He played Nick Nack on my tree, etc.

4. This old man,
   He played four,
   He played Nick Nack on my door, etc.

5. . . . . .
   He played Nick Nack on my drive, etc.

6. . . . . .
   He played Nick Nack on my sticks, etc.

7. . . . . .
   He played Nick Nack up to heaven, etc.

8. . . . . .
   He played Nick Nack on my gate, etc.

9. . . . . .
   He played Nick Nack down the line.

10. . . . . .
    He played Nick Nack with my hen, etc.

COLOR-IN CARMEN

Ask Mother or Dad if they have a record of the "Habanera" from the opera CARMEN by Georges Bizet. In the opera, the Gypsy girl, Carmen, sings this song as she dances and plays the castanets. Listen carefully to the rhythm, and then try to dance and play along with her. In fact, the whole rhythm band can play.

Here is a picture of Carmen dancing. Color it in. Try to use the bright colors that you think Spanish Gypsies might wear.

KNOCK-KNOCK PAGE

Mr. Moose: Knock-knock.
Captain: Who's there?
Mr. Moose: Rumford.
Captain: Rumford who?
Mr. Moose: Rumford the hills, here they come!

Mr. Moose: Knock-knock.
Captain: Who's there?
Mr. Moose: Wendy.
Captain: Wendy who?
Mr. Moose: Wendy moon comes over de mountain, I'll be dropping ping-pong balls on you.

Mr. Moose: Knock-knock.
Captain: Who's there?
Mr. Moose: Arthur and Esther.
Captain: Arthur and Esther who?
Mr. Moose: Arthur any more ping-pong balls up there?

16

Here is a playtime project with empty containers

CONTAINER TOWN

You can make your own town if you save up empty milk, cream, margarine, and ice cream containers—and cereal and cookie boxes.

Standing upright, a milk carton can be an office building or apartment house. On its side, it becomes a row of stores. A cereal box laid flat may be a supermarket or department store. Cream cartons (or milk cartons cut in half) make good houses.

Margarine containers, stacked on top of each other could be a parking garage—or a modern art museum! And empty yogurt containers are great ice cream drive-ins.

All you have to do is to cover the containers with construction paper and decorate them any way you like. Maybe your village will look something like this one.

STARFISH

There is a strange creature
That lives in the sea.
He's just as unusual
As a creature can be.
He looks like a star
With his arms stretched out
So we call him a Starfish
(Instead of a Trout).

He comes in bright colors,
Especially red,
And he looks very strange
'Cause he hasn't a head.
But he does have a mouth
In a very odd place,
It's tucked underneath . . .
'Cause he hasn't a face.

He searches the bottom for something to eat,
The mussels and clams make a wonderful treat.
He pulls their shells open and gobbles them up,
Then looks for some oysters on which he can sup,.

There's just one more thing that I think you should
know
If he loses an arm, the starfish can grow
Another new arm to put in its place. . . .
Still, he hasn't a head . . .
And he hasn't a face!

Susan Birkenhead

JOKE PAGE

Captain: What happened when the duck flew upside down?
Mr. Moose: He quacked up.

Captain: Why did the elephant stand on the marshmallow?
Mr. Moose: So he wouldn't fall into the cocoa.

Captain: What's black and white and red all over?
Mr. Moose: A sunburned zebra.

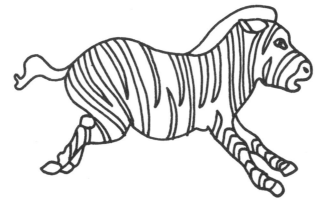

IF YOU HAPPEN TO BE A CAT

If you happen to be a cat,
Most any kind of cat,
With paws and fur—
A him or a her,
You've got a tongue that's rough and pink.
And I certainly think
it goes without saying
that you do a lot of playing.
And you primp and you preen
All through the day
And you lick yourself clean
In your own special way.
You'll surely do all that—
If you're a cat.

If you happen to be a cat
Most any kind of cat
With the usual ears and fur,
You have a pleasant purr
And time to spend with a friend.

You have lots of curiosity
Especially when you see
Something strange and new
There are lots of things to do
And lots of things to see
If you happen to be . . .
a cat.

Stan Davis

Here's a playtime store that you can have lots of rainy day fun with

PLAYTIME STORE

First you'll need a large cardboard carton for the counter. Decorate it with signs advertising your "specials."

For your cash register, take a shoebox, turn it on one side and force the top into it like this—

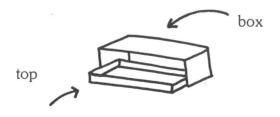

—this will be your cash drawer.

Put your cash register on the top of your counter.

Ask Mother for small, empty boxes, or plastic bottles that can be your merchandise—which means the things that you will sell.

Now you have everything except . . . . . money. Here's how to make that.

Borrow a penny, a nickel, a dime, and a quarter. Then trace their shapes as many times as you want on to cardboard and cut them out. Number each cardboard coin according to its proper value: ① for a penny, ⑤ for a nickel, ⑩ for a dime, and ㉕ for a quarter.

Now, take sheets of green construction paper (or any paper about that size) and fold each piece in half the short way—

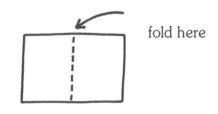

fold here

—then into thirds, the other way—

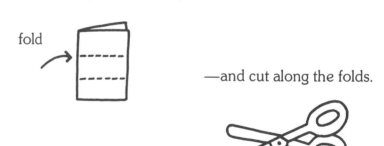

fold

—and cut along the folds.

For each sheet of paper you will have six "bills". Label four of them $1.00 and two of them $5.00 .

Now you are ready to open your store. Maybe Mother or an older brother or sister will be your first customer and help you to learn about money and how to make change.

21

WHY BUNNY RABBITS EAT CARROTS

Once upon a time, in far off Rabbit Forest there lived a fine young rabbit named, Bunny. Bunny was a good rabbit. He always put away his toys and kept his room neat and clean. He said "Yes'm" and "Yes, sir," and never forgot "Please" and "Thank you." In fact, he was so good that his mother, Mrs. Rabbit, had only one problem—hamburgers!

That's right. The only food that Bunny would eat was . . . . . hamburgers.

When Mrs. Rabbit would serve her finest fresh lettuce or cabbage or turnip greens, Bunny would say—very politely—"No thank you, Ma'am, I'll have a hamburger, if you please."

Of course hamburgers are fine food, but growing bunnies must eat lots of vegetables, too; so one day Mrs. Rabbit said, "Bunny, no more hamburgers until you eat your greens . . . . . and that is final!" And Mr. Rabbit said, "Final, indeed!"

That evening, when the lettuce was passed, Bunny said, "No thank you, Ma'am," as politely as he could, hoping that his mother would change her mind. But

Mr. and Mrs. Rabbit could not go back on their word, so Bunny had no dinner at all.

The next day it was the same . . . and the day after that. Bunny got hungrier and hungrier; but still he would say, "No thank you, Ma'am," when the greens were passed. Soon he was so hungry that he could think of nothing but hamburgers. He even dreamed about hamburgers at night.

Then one day, as Bunny was hopping slowly down Rabbit Road, trying not to think of food, he came upon a moose who was stuck in mud right up to his nose. Bunny was very weak from not eating, but with his last bit of strength he pulled the moose free.

Gratefully, the moose said, "Oh thank you, brave bunny. What can I do to repay you for saving me?"

"Hamburgers," said Bunny. "I must have hamburgers!"

"You are in luck," said the moose. "I am Paul Beaumousse, chef to the king. I shall take you to the royal palace and you shall have all the hamburgers you can eat!"

And so it was. The moose began to make hamburgers and the rabbit ate them as fast as the moose could make them.

Time marched on!

Chef Beaumousse tried to get Bunny to eat other foods: spinach, lettuce, cabbage, fish, chicken. But Bunny would just say (politely), "No thank you, sir; I'll have more hamburgers , if you please."

Finally the moose tossed his antlers in despair. "I can't go on," he said. "I am very grateful to Bunny Rabbit, but I cannot *look* at one more hamburger. What am I to do? This rabbit will eat nothing but hamburgers!"

The moose thought and thought. Finally, he hit upon a plan. The next morning, when the rabbit came for his breakfast, the moose said, "I'm sorry, Bunny, but you will have to wait for your hamburgers. I am preparing a very special birthday feast for our Wise Old King."

"Is it hamburger? " said Bunny.

"Heavens, no!" said the chef. On his birthday, the king has a SPECIAL FEAST FOR WISE OLD KINGS. It is a magic food that keeps him wise all year!

"Magic food," said Bunny. "Oh, please, may I have some, Chef Beaumousse?"

The moose thought a while. Then he said, "This MAGIC FOOD *is* only for the king . . . but you *did* save my life and I *am* grateful. I would give you some . . . but, no. You wouldn't like it."

"Oh yes, yes. I'm sure I would like MAGIC FOOD," said Bunny. "Please!"

"No," said the moose. "You like only hamburgers."

But the more the moose insisted that the rabbit would not like the MAGIC FOOD, the more the rabbit insisted on trying it. Finally the moose said, "Oh, allright. I know you won't like it, but here it is. It's called a CARROT and it grows in the ground."

So Bunny took a bite. It was good! He ate the whole carrot, and then another. He even ate the greens at the top! Then the happy moose showed Bunny where the carrots grew so that he could have as many as he wanted.

"Oh thank you, Chef Beaumousse," said Bunny. "Thank you for everything . . . especially for the MAGIC CARROTS; but I must go home now. My mother and father will be worried."

So Bunny gathered as many bunches of carrots as he could carry and set out for home.

Mr. and Mrs. Rabbit were so happy to see their Bunny that they even offered him a hamburger; but to their surprise, he said, "No thank you, Ma'am; no thank you, Sir. I have a MAGIC FOOD that *you* must try." And they did try the carrots and they all liked them.

That night, when the greens were passed, Bunny said, "Thank you, Ma'am. I think I'll try some with my carrots." And he did; and they were good!

So, you see, the carrots *were* magical, after all; and they *did* make Bunny wise. Because, from that time to this, he has tried whatever Mrs. Rabbit has put on his plate. And now, he likes *almost* everything . . . including hamburgers.

Bob Colleary

23

This is a poem that is called a "patter song". That means that instead of singing it, you talk it in a rhythmic way. Try clapping your hands or using your rhythm band instruments. It may take some practice, but it will be great fun. Ready—1, 2, 3, 4—

"THREE SQUARES A DAY"

Now listen to me children, I got something to say
Eat three square meals ev'ry day
    Three square meals ev'ry day
    Yeah, Yeah, Yeah!

Let's start out with breakfast and see what we got
There's juice and cereal and toast that's hot
There's gotta be milk and maybe some ham
And on that toast throw a little bit o' jam
    On that toast throw a little bit o' jam
    Yeah, Yeah, Yeah!

Now as time goes on, we begin to droop
So start that lunch with a little bit o' soup
There's milk and fruit and my heart goes a flutter

When I dig that sandwich o' peanut butter
    Dig that sandwich o' peanut butter
    Yeah, Yeah, Yeah!

Now moving right along to the evening meal
Try chicken and beef or maybe some veal
There's one more thing before we split the scene
If you wanna stay healthy you gotta think green
    You wanna stay healthy you gotta think green
    Yeah, Yeah, Yeah!

That's three square meals and they shouldn't be missed
No more questions? Class is dismissed.
    Yeah, Yeah, Yeah!

Bob Colleary

Here are two playtime projects that use sound to have fun.

OLD FASHIONED RADIO

You'll need a small cardboard box about the size of a shoebox, an empty cardboard tube from a paper towel or aluminum foil roll (the longer the better), a piece of foil, and a paper cup.

First, ask a grown-up to cut a hole in the bottom of the cup just big enough to fit the tube.

Slip the cup over the end of the tube. It should fit tightly.

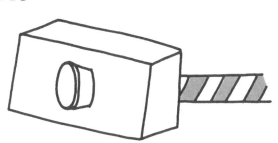

Draw a dial and some knobs on your radio and you're finished.

To "play" the radio, put your mouth to the end of the tube and talk or sing. Your voice will sound as though it were coming from an old-fashioned radio or phonograph.

Now, tape the piece of foil *loosely* over the top of the cup.

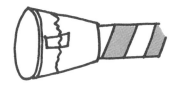

Then, have a hole cut in the bottom of the box so that the cup will fit into it tightly. Slip the tube through this hole, from the outside of the box, until the cup is firmly held in place.

Put on an old time radio show for Mom and Dad. Try singing some old-fashioned songs. The grown-ups will help you with the tunes.

Dot·to·Dot

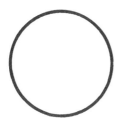

Where is Dancing Bear? Follow the dots in order and you'll see.

THE CAMEL

The camel is a strange and awkward beast
To say the least.
He lives in the deserts of Africa and Asia,
Some things about him might amaze ya!

He has three eyelids on each eye
And heavy brows. Do you know why
The lashes on his eyes are long
And his nose can close when the wind is strong?

Such things were planned by Nature's hand
To keep out sand in desert land.

When food is scarce in desert drought,
He does without.
For the hump on his back is filled with fat.
He uses that.

The camel doesn't like his work.
He moans and groans, but doesn't shirk.
He carries loads where there are no roads,
In places where a car or truck
Would certainly get very stuck.

The desert life is hard, of course,
And man can't make it with his horse;
But luckily for desert man
He has a camel caravan.

Stan Davis

PAPER CUP TELEPHONES

You need 2 paper cups, 2 buttons, and a long piece of string. Have someone punch a tiny hole in the bottom of each cup. Thread the ends of the string through the holes and tie a button to each end.

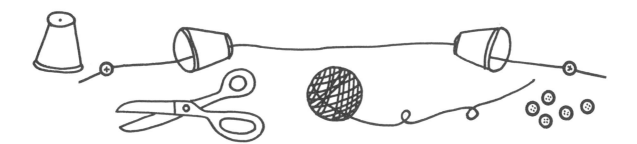

Pull the string so that the buttons are against the inside of the cup bottoms.

To make a "phone call", hold one cup and have a friend take the other. Important: hold the cups at their tops with just one finger and thumb.

Do not wrap your hand around the cup; it will muffle the sound.

Stretch the string tight between the cups. Talk into your cup while your friend listens to his. Then put your cup to your ear and have your friend talk into his. The sound will travel along the string from the talker to the listener. With a long enough string you can talk from one room to another; but remember the string must be stretched tight in order for your phones to work.

A NATURE WALK

Is there a park near where you live? Or do you live in the country where there are fields and trees everywhere? No matter where you live, there is bound to be some place, not far away, where you can learn some of the wonderful secrets of nature.

Ask Mother and Dad to take you on a "Nature Walk". Instead of running and playing, walk slowly and look around you. See how many things—little things—you can find that you never noticed before.

Look at the ground. Look closely. What do you see.

Animals

A hop toad? All bumpy and brown with black spots.

If you hadn't looked closely you wouldn't have seen it. It looks just like the little rocks. That's how it hides from its enemies.

And there's a chipmunk hiding in the brown leaves.

Insects

What's that? A blade of grass? A twig? No, it moved! It's a praying mantis . It, too, hides by looking just like the things around it. And so do the grasshopper and the inch worm . But if you look very closely, you can find them.

Rocks

What about those rocks and pebbles? Are they all the same? No! Collect as many different kinds as you can. Take them home and sort them. When you go to the library, ask for a book on rocks. See if you can find pictures of *your* rocks. Then you'll know what kinds you have. An empty egg crate is a good place to keep your collection.

Leaves

Look at the leaves on the trees. In summer they are all green—but are they all the same? No. Each kind of tree has a different shaped leaf. Collect some. Take them home and press them between the pages of a book. Put something heavy on top of the book. In about five days your leaves will be dry and you can paste them on paper to make a leaf scrap book.

30

Crayon Prints

You can make pretty crayon prints of your leaves, too. Just put a piece of plain paper on top of a leaf, then rub a crayon over the paper. Magically, the outline and veins of the leaf will appear on the paper. Make prints of different kinds of leaves in different colors. These will make a good scrapbook, too.

Identify Your Leaves

Look at the shapes of your leaves. They will tell you what kinds of trees they came from:

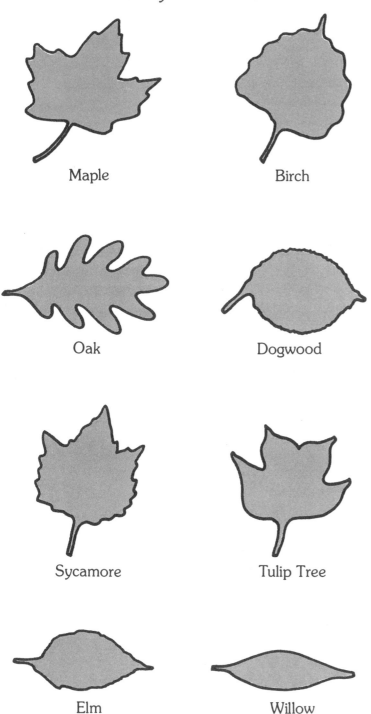

Maple

Birch

Oak

Dogwood

Sycamore

Tulip Tree

Elm

Willow

Compare your leaves with these drawings. Then label the leaves in your book.

Seeds

At certain times of the year you will see the seeds of the trees. Some seeds have wings so that the wind will carry them to distant places to become new trees. They look like this:

If there are squirrels around sit quietly and watch them. They may be gathering acorns for their food supply. The acorn is the seed of the oak tree. It is a large seed, but it seems very small when you think that someday it may grow into a huge oak tree a hundred or more feet tall.

I hope you'll like your nature walks. There are so many wonderful things to see and learn. And they're all put there by Nature for us to enjoy—and to treasure . . . and respect. Remember that animals, plants, rocks, and water are all our partners on this wonderful Earth. We must take care not to destroy these precious gifts.

"The world is so full of a number of things,
I'm sure we should all be as happy as kings."

31

How would you like to make puppets of me and Bun? O.K. here's how

PUPPETS

Bunny Rabbit

You'll need an old cloth glove (grown-up size), a 2½" styrofoam or soft rubber ball, a piece of cloth about the size of a handkerchief, an old pencil with a point and some glue or tape.

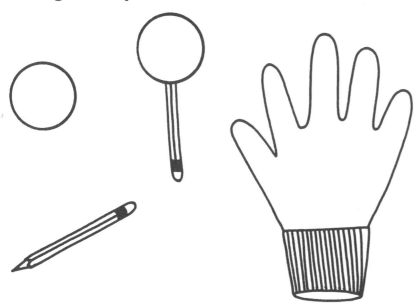

First, stick the pencil into the ball to make a handle. Then, stuff the ball as far into the glove as it will go. Next, tape or pin the pointer finger of the glove down in the back (the side opposite the palm of the glove) . . . like this

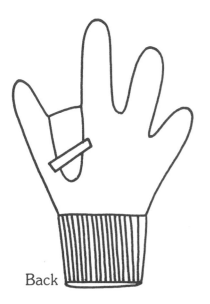

Back

Front

Now turn the glove so that the palm faces you. You will see that the remaining fingers form Bunny's ears and arms.

Trace these on a piece of stiff paper and cut them out, (you may need help). Bend the arms back and glue or tape them to the sides of Bunny's head.

With felt pens of sharp crayons, draw the eyes, nose, and mouth—or you might want to paste on a circle of colored paper for the nose.

Cloth

Now hold the piece of cloth by its center and cut off the top to form a hole just big enough to fit over the bottom of the glove.

Slip the bottom of the glove (with the pencil inside) through the hole and tie a string around the cloth to hold it tight.

Now you can slip your hand up under the cloth to hold your puppet.

32

Mr. Moose Puppet

You'll need an old sock—light brown color is best, a piece of cloth about the size of a handkerchief, a 2½" styrofoam or soft rubber ball, a pencil with a point, two pipe cleaners, white glue, felt tipped pens or sharp crayons.

First, stuff the cloth all the way up to the toe of the sock to form my long, handsome snout.

Then stick the pencil into the ball to form a handle and push the ball up into the sock behind the cloth to make the rest of my noble head.

Now trace these antlers on a piece of paper, color them —yellow—and cut them out.

Take the two pipe cleaners and bend them to look like this ◁───. Paste the triangles to the uncolored side of the antlers, leaving the straight ends of the cleaners sticking out at the bottom.

Push the antlers into my noble head, ouch— gently!—making sure that the paper sides face forward.

Trace my eyes and nose, and ears, on paper, cut them out, and paste them where you think they should go. Finally, draw my mouth and presto, you have a Mr. Moose puppet to play with your Bunny Rabbit puppet.

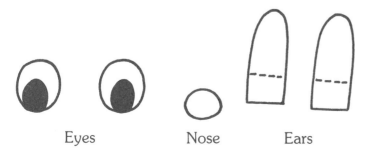

Eyes   Nose   Ears

Worm Puppets

Ask Mom for another old pair of socks—light brown is the best color. Put your hand—with fingers straight out—into the sock as far as it will go.

Toe   Heel

Now spread your thumb away from your fingers and push the toe of the sock in between your fingers and thumb.

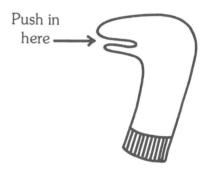

Push in here ➝

Next, clamp your thumb against your fingers to hold the pushed in part of the stock. Pull the sock off your hand (inside out) but hold on to the part between your thumb and fingers.

Let go of the sock and ask Mother to sew right across the end of that folded part that you were holding.

Sew here.

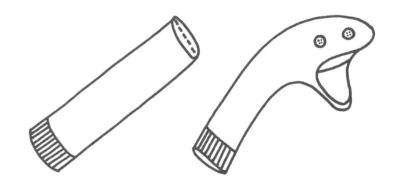

Turn the sock rightside out, have Mom sew on buttons for the eyes, and you have your worm puppet.

These puppets are great fun for singing along with records or television.

COLOR-IN LION

PIPE CLEANER PEOPLE AND ANIMALS

Have you ever made pipe cleaner figures? They're easy to make and lots of fun to play with. All you need are some pipe cleaners (which will cost about 15 cents) and some heavy scissors for cutting them. Kitchen shears are good for this—if you have permission to use them—but *please* not Mom's best scissors. Ask an older person to help you with this project. You'll both have fun making stick figures from pipe cleaners.

Try making people first. Here's how:

1. Bend a pipe cleaner over a pencil so that both ends of the cleaner are the same length.

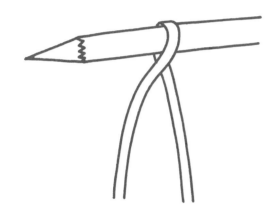

2. Twist the ends together about four times, keeping them equal in length.
3. Now remove the pencil from the loop it has formed. Your figure should look like this.

4. Next, take another pipe cleaner and twist it around your figure just below the head loop . . . like this:

5. Bend the arms down to the sides and have someone cut them to proper arm length . . . about one inch.
6. Now, all you have to do is bend the very bottoms of the legs forward to make the feet . . . and, PRESTO, you have a pipe cleaner person!

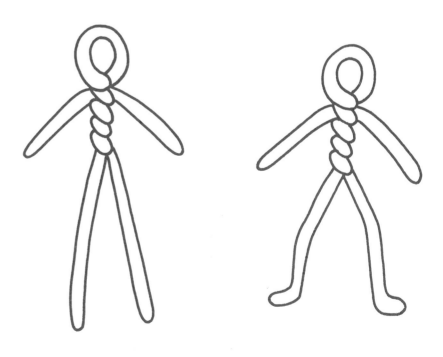

I think you'll find him a good playmate. You can bend his arms, legs, and body to make him:

SIT WALK RUN THROW

—or whatever you like.

But do make a friend for him so he won't get lonely when you're not around.

Of course, you can also make pipe cleaner animals, like this Longhorn Steer.

Use one cleaner for the head, backbone, and tail . . .

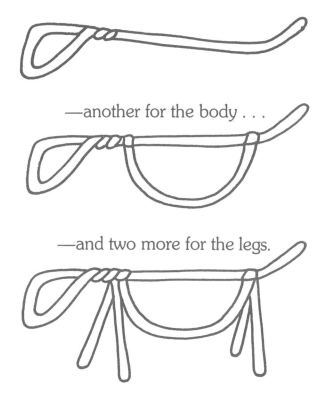

—another for the body . . .

—and two more for the legs.

Then, twist a two-and-a-half inch length of cleaner through the head loop and bend the ends up to form the longhorns.

Now, if you want, you can make one of your people figures into a cowboy by putting him on the back of the steer and having him ride in a rodeo.

Of course you can make other animals like elephants . . .

—giraffes . . .

—or even a camel.

Or you can make things for your people to play with, like this swing:

See how many things you can think of to make, yourself.

This is good fun for a rainy day.

37

THE LITTLE FAMILY

Now that you know how to make pipe cleaner people, here's a way that you can have your own Little Family.

Here are bodies for Lydia, Lorenzo and Uncle Leander.

Lydia

Lorenzo

Uncle Leander

Color them with crayons or felt-tipped pens and cut them out. (You may want to ask for help with the cutting.) Then, take three pipe cleaner figures and paste the Little Family cut-outs to them with white glue.

Now you have the Little Family . . . but they have no place to live. Sooooo . . .

Ask Mom if she has a shoebox—or any small cardboard box—to use as their house. You might want to crayon some designs on the inside walls to look like wallpaper.

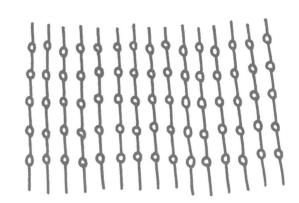

Now cut *used* stamps from old envelopes and paste them to the walls for pictures.

A photograph of a rug, cut from a magazine, can be pasted to the floor.

Of course, the Littles use whatever tiny things they can find for furniture.

Plastic caps from old toothpaste or shampoo tubes make good stools.

An empty thread spool with a flat plastic container top pasted to it is a perfect table.

Small, *empty* matchboxes (*make sure there are no matches in them*) pasted on top of each other make fine dressers and chests.

And the inside part of a matchbox or any small, open box, filled with cotton and covered with a piece of scrap cloth is a very fine bed.

See if you can find other small objects around the house that would make good furniture.

When you've finished your Little Family house, find a *special* place to keep it . . . maybe your bookshelf (where the Littles live in the Captain's Place) or on a closet shelf . . . some place secret, because the Littles do like privacy.

Oh, and please don't tell Mr. Moose or Bunny Rabbit, or Mr. Greenjeans—*or anyone*—about the Little Family. Remember, they're our secret.

Here's a picture of the Little's house to guide you. You may color it in if you like.

THE GREAT CARROT DELIVERY GAME

The object of this game is to deliver the carrots (your button) from Mr. Greenjeans' barn to the Captain's Place.

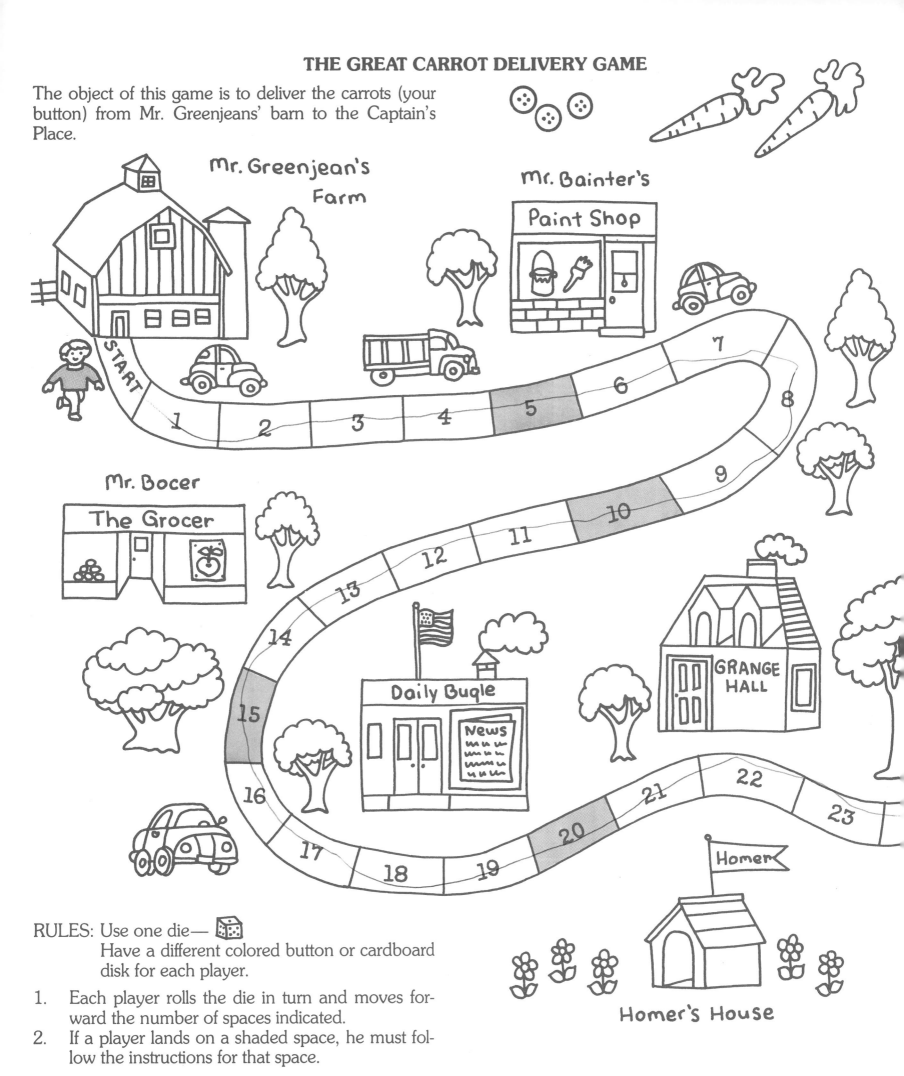

RULES: Use one die—
      Have a different colored button or cardboard disk for each player.

1. Each player rolls the die in turn and moves forward the number of spaces indicated.
2. If a player lands on a shaded space, he must follow the instructions for that space.

Instructions For Shaded Spaces

5—Carrot trick—back to start.

10—Take ride in Mercy—go forward 3 spaces.

15—Mercy breaks down—go back 4 spaces.

20—Stop to help Homer find buried bone—go back 3 spaces.

25—Instant Trip-izer sends you ahead 4 spaces.

30—Jog along with Mr. Baxter—go forward 4 spaces.

35—Get help from Dennis—go back 3 spaces.

40—Play hide-and-seek with Dancing Bear—go back 4 spaces.

45—Instant trip-izer broken—go back 4 spaces.

50—Ping-pong balls on road—go back 3 spaces.

55—Captain is sleeping—go back 7 spaces.

THE ZEBRA

The zebra's a cousin of the horse;
But, unlike the horse, the zebra, of course,
Is wild and fierce and hard to tame.
And the first thing you think of when you hear
his name . . . is stripes!

There are several different zebra types,
But all the zebra types have stripes.

Such bold designs of dark and light!
Are they white on black . . . or black on white?
I think the answer is the latter,
But to the zebra it doesn't matter

Stan Davis

© *Saugatuck Productions*

I think they're black on white

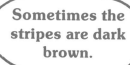

Sometimes the stripes are dark brown.

The stripes help him to hide from his enemy, the lion.

The zebra comes from Africa.

THE LADYBUG

The prettiest bug I ever did see
Was crawling around on the leaf of a tree.
All shiny and red with polka dot wings,
The Lady Bird Beetle she's called of all things!

The prettiest bug, the friendliest too,
She's helpful to farmers and gardeners who
Can use her to rid them of bugs that would harm
The plants in the garden and crops on the farm.

Lady Bird, Lady Bird, fly away, fly.
Unfold your wings and take to the sky.
Lady Bird, Lady Bird fly away home
Just like the Lady Bird bug in the poem.

Thanks from the farmer for saving his trees.
Thanks from the gardener, too, if you please.
And one special thank you, a kiss and a hug
From me, for just being a pretty red bug.

Susan Birkenhead

I use ladybugs to protect the roses in the Captain's Place.

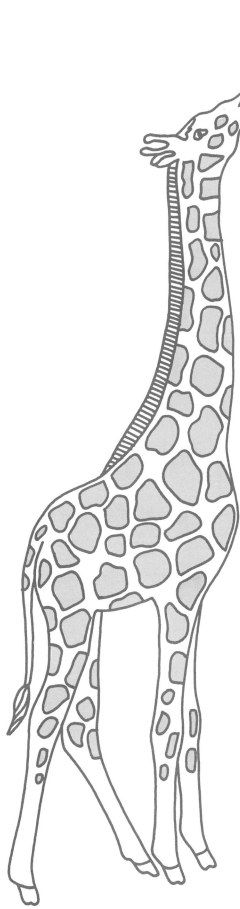

THE GIRAFFE

The giraffe is the tallest of all wild creatures,
And his neck is the strangest of all his features.
He's able to reach way up with ease
    Whenever he's
Nibbling the leaves in the trees.

The giraffe has a tongue twenty inches long.
It's used like a hand—it's very strong—
To reach out for food when he's in the mood
And he hears his tummy dinner bell chime,
And that means practically any old time.

He eats much faster than people do,
And that's because he doesn't chew.
He gulps it all down, every leaf and bud,
And he'll chew it later when he chews his cud.

When he wants water or when he's found
Something he'd like to reach on the ground,
His front legs stretch out wide to each side
He couldn't stretch them more if he tried.

Reaching his neck down in between
He looks so long and lean,
As awkward as a newborn calf,
But please, dear friends, don't laugh—
Don't laugh . . .

At the gentle, Gentle giraffe.

Stan Davis

BLIMP

Blow up a long, sausage type balloon and tie it off. Take a long narrow cookie or cracker box and on it draw windows and doors. Now tape the box to the underside of the balloon to form the blimp's cabin—which is called a gondola. Tape a string—for a mooring line—to the nose of the blimp, and there you have it. If you like, give your blimp a name and print it on the balloon with a magic marker.

AQUARIUM

Take a shoebox and cut a big window in the bottom. Stretch a piece of cellophane or plastic wrap across the inside of the opening and paste it to the inside of the box. Cut a long narrow slit in one side of the box.

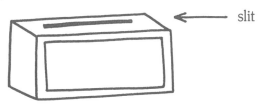

← slit

Set the box on its side so that the slit is on top. Make underwater plants from construction paper and tape them to the "ocean floor". Put some small rocks among them.

Draw an underwater scene on the inside of the box top, and then tape the top in place.

Now you have an underwater world but you need some creatures to move around in it. So . . . draw different kinds of fish and maybe a diver on construction paper, cut them out and paste a pipe cleaner to each one. These are your undersea puppets. Pass them through the slit and move them about in your underwater theater.

pipe cleaners

44

PARTY PAGES

Paper Bag Relay Race

For this one you will need lots of paper bags—not *too* big. Have the group line up in two teams at one end of the room. At the opposite end of the room, put piles of small paper bags (one bag for each player) on two chairs.

At the starting signal, the first player on each team runs to his chair, takes a paper bag, blows it up, bursts it, and runs back to touch the next player on his team—who then takes his turn—and so on. The first team to finish wins.

Balloon Relay

You'll need two blown-up, round balloons for this race—plus some spares in case of burstings.

Players form two teams at one end of the room. One chair is placed at the other end of the room. A balloon is put on the floor in front of each team at the starting line. At the word "Go" the first players must drop to their hands and knees and blow their balloons across the room to the chair, through the chair legs, and back to the starting line where the next player takes over.

Remember, the balloons must not be touched with the hands. If a balloon should burst, the player must go back to the starting line and begin again with a new balloon.

Mum Bird and Don't Laugh

After all that excitement it might be a good idea for everyone to sit down in a circle and rest up with a quiet game called "Mum Bird". You see, a "Mum Bird" never says a word—and that's the object of the game: not to speak. The players sit in a circle and look at each other—but try not to say a word! It sounds easy, doesn't it? But try it! It's a lot harder than you think. The person who can stay quiet the longest wins.

An even harder variation of this game is called "Don't Laugh". In this one you can neither talk nor laugh. This one is so hard that almost no one can last as long as a minute.

Story Relay

Here's another sitting game, the "Story Relay". The first player begins telling a story, making it up as he goes along. It can be any sort of story he likes.

For example, player #1 might begin: "I have a white cat named Wilfred. One day Wilfred was walking down the street when he met a huge, ferocious . . ."

Player #1 stops at this point and the next player must continue the story. If he wants to be serious he could begin ". . . dog, who was carrying a big bone". But if he wants the story to be funny, he might say ". . . mouse, eight feet tall, who grew that big because he had eaten . . ."

Now it's the third player's turn. He might begin with ". . . a watermelon seed . . ." and so on around the circle of players.

Another way to play this game is to have a box full of small objects such as a spoon, a candle, an apple, a sponge, a toy airplane, a rubber spider . . . anything that might make a funny story—the sillier the better.

As each player's turn comes around, he closes his eyes and takes an object from the box. His part of the story must have something to do with the object he has chosen.

Try it, it's a good way to get some crazy mixed-up stories.

Here are some Hallowe'en costumes that are easy to make and fun to wear.

HALLOWE'EN COSTUMES

Paper Bag Costumes

Find a paper bag just big enough around to fit snugly over your head . . . not too tight. Put it on and have someone mark lightly where your eyes, nose, and mouth come on the bag. Take the bag off and draw a funny face on it, keeping the eyes, nose, and mouth in the right places. Then, ask a grown-up to cut holes for the eyes and mouth, and cut around the sides and bottom of the nose—but not across the top. Ear flaps can also be cut in the sides or top.

Color the mask in bright tones. Make it funny or scary. If you have some yellow yarn, you can paste it on top for hair.

Here is a Dancing Bear mask that Dennis made.

If you can find a bag big enough to fit over your shoulders, draw clothes on it, cut a hole in the top for your head and one in each side for your arms. Slip it on before you put your mask on.

Or—if you can find a *really* big bag that comes all the way down to your knees, draw a *big* face, using the whole length of the bag. Make the cut-out eyes come where your eyes are so that you will be able to see, but don't cut out the mouth and nose because they'll be way down at your waist. People will really laugh at this costume.

Here's an important rule: never, never use a plastic bag for a mask

48

Make-believe Spectacles

You'll need four pipe cleaners. Bend two into circles like this

leaving an end sticking out on each one. Now twist the ends together.

Bend the other two to fit over your ears and twist them onto the frames.

If you have colored cellophane you can cut out "lenses" and paste them to your frames to make sunglasses.

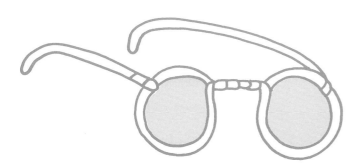

Moustache and Beard

Draw a shape like this on a piece of cardboard.

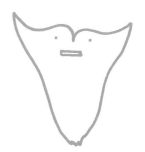

Make it big enough to fit your mouth.

Have a grown-up cut it out and punch the two holes shown. Thread a piece of string through the holes. This is to tie it to your head.

Take absorbent cotton and paste it to your cut-out and you will have an old man's white beard and moustache to wear with your glasses.

Stocking Mask

Here's a quick way to change your appearance. Ask Mother for an old nylon stocking. Pull it down over your head. It will change all your features. Move it around until you get the funniest effect.

Dot·to·Dot

Remember: follow the dots in order, 1 to 30.

CAPTAIN KANGAROO'S ALPHABET

A a

"A" is for antlers,
A moose has two.
"A" is for apple
And aardvark stew.

B b

Bunny's name begins with "B"
Bunny—bug—buzz—bite—bump—
    bandage

C c

"C" is for Captain and carrot.
When Bunny wants a carrot,
The tricks are soon started;
And the Captain and his carrots
Are very soon parted.

D d

"D" is for Debbie.
Debbie is dreaming that she's
dancing on a drum.

Dance Debbie, Dance!

E e

"E" is for elephant . . .
—and eensie-weensie.

Enormous!

F f

"F" is for frog and friends.

A froggie did
a flirting go.

fee foh fiddle fie

fum

G g

"G" is for Greenjeans.
Mr. Greenjeans grows great green beans in his by-golly jolly green garden!

H h

"H" is for Homer.
Homer hound is hard to please.
His howl is so forlorn!
But if you give his nose a squeeze,
It honks just like a horn.

Homer, you're my hero!

Honk

hoooo

I i

"I" is for ice, igloo, iguana.

An iguana in an igloo?

Leapin' Lizards!

An iguana is a lizard.

J j

"J" is for Jennifer.
Jennifer likes jelly and jam,
but enjoys her juice just as much!

K k

"K" is for kangaroo.
When the kangaroo kissed
the king in the kitchen,
the kitten kicked the kettle . . .

Kerplunk

L l

"L" is for Lydia Little.
Look at Lydia Little
on a ladder, licking a
lollipop!

Lime! How luscious.

Lydia
loves
lollipops

"M" stands for Mister and Moose.
The first "M" for Mister,
The second for Moose,
If the second were "G",
He'd be Mister Goose.

Honk, honk!

Who's there?

"N" stands for nap and nod.
Shh! no noise—no rapping or tapping.
Grandfather Clock is busy, napping.
He likes to nod, both night and noon,
In bright sunshine or light of moon.

Let's see if we can waken him— ready: 1-2-3— "Hello Grandfather"

Wh-what? Oh . . . . . Nighty— night.

"O" is for oats, over, order-

Over and out!

and hay!

Hay!!??

O.K. Bun he ordered it!

Oh, oh!

P p

"P" is for ping,
"P" is for pong,
"P" is for Preston.

Preston who?

Preston the button—and down they come!

Q q

"Q" is for question.
Question: What did Quincy Quail say to
　　　　　Quenton Duck when the hunter
　　　　　came close?
Answer: Quick, Quenton, quit quacking!

Uncle Leander, did you know that "q" is always followed by "u"?

Not by me! I quit!

Quite

Dat's quazy!

R r

"R" is for rabbit, rooster, robin,
rose, Robert. Rabbit, rooster, and
Robert played Ring-around-the-Roses.

S s

"S" is for:
ship—sail—sea—storm—

—saved!

T t

"T" is for tic-tac-toe.
Tiny-tiny Tina plays
Tic-tac-toe
With Too-tall Tom.

Tom's
Terrific

U u

"U" is for uncle, umbrella, up.

Uncle Leander,
what goes up the
chimney down—
but won't go down
the chimney up?

Easy!
An umbrella.

And don't
call me
Uncle

V v

"V" is for Valentine.

To Homer—

Vines are green,
Violets are blue,
Vegetables are
good for me...
—And so
are
You!!

—from
~~Jennifer~~
Guess who!

I ♥ LOVE YOU

Very embarrassing

Smack

W w

"W" is for wind and winter.
There's wind in the willows and wind on the hill.
The window shade whips with its cord at the sill.
The wild geese are winging their way through the sky.
Soon winter will whistle its cold lullaby.

Wow! What a wild wind, Wilfred

Wight on Wabbit

X x

"X" marks the spot where the treasure is buried.
I went to find the hidden box,
And took an ax to break the locks.
I met an ox and foxes too;
But could not find the mystery clue.

Extra Extra Box Outfoxes Moose

EXTRA

?

N E + W S

Here are two easy Playtimes for bathtub fun

MILK CARTON OCEAN LINER

Thoroughly wash out an empty milk carton—either quart or half gallon size. Lay it on one side so that the pointed top is running up and down.

Make sure that the place where it was opened is at the top. Otherwise your boat may sink!

Ask Mother to cut a toilet paper tube in half with a bread knife or scissors. *Do not do this yourself. Never use sharp knives yourself.*

cut here

Tape the two tubes to the top of the milk carton. These are the smoke stacks for your liner.

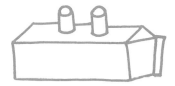

Take your ship with you when you take a bath. It will float—and provide lots of fun.

Another good bathtub boat starts with a large bath-size cake of soap that *floats*. Next take a wooden lolly-pop stick (or pencil) and sharpen one end in a pencil sharpener. Stick the pointed end in (but not through) the soap.

Cut a big triangle from a piece of construction paper and fold it in half to make a smaller triangle.

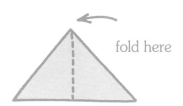

fold here

Paste this sail around your lolli-pop stick mast so that it points out to one corner of the soap bar.

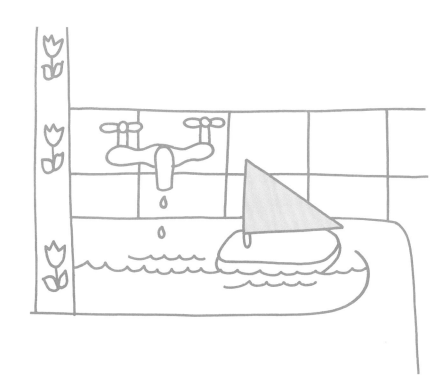

Float the boat in the bathtub. When you blow against the sail, the boat will move. Try blowing from the back, the side, and even the front. You may be surprised at the way your boat moves.

When you go to the library, ask for a book about sailing and sailing ships. You'll learn how people for thousands of years have used the wind to move their boats on rivers, lakes, and oceans—just as you can move yours in the bathtub.

Here are some poems with the last word missing. Can you find the right word to finish the rhyme?

FINISH THE RHYME

Oh, I can do just as I choose—
I'm such a clever "fella".
I make you wear your overshoes
And open your umbrella.
I make the grass grow green and tall,
I flood the plain in Spain;
And push the mighty waterfall,
I call myself the _____.

Down through the dark night sky I fall;
Silently I cover all
The earth and houses far below
With a soft, white blanket.
I'm the _____.

I wake you in the morning
As in the east I rise.
So bright am I at noontime
That you must shade your eyes.
I paint the western sky at dusk
To say that day is done,
At night you cannot see me,
I am your friend the _____.

Sometimes I'm just a sliver,
Sometimes, I'm half a ball;
Sometimes, I'm big and round and bright,
Sometimes, not there at all.
Sometimes I float above the trees
Just like a big balloon,
Next time you see me, holler please,
"Hello, there, Mr. _____."

"Tick-tock, tick-tock,"
Grandfather Clock.
"Ding-dong, ding-dong,"
Grandfather's song.
Daytime, nighttime,
Grandfather keeps
ticking, tocking
While he _____.

1. rain 2. snow 3. sun 4. moon 5. sleeps

61

WINDMILL

Here is a neat thing you can do with an empty milk carton. You'll probably want to ask for some help on this one. We're going to make an *Old-Fashioned Dutch Windmill.*

Here are the materials you'll need:

A thoroughly washed out, empty one-quart milk carton.
A drinking straw.
Three pipe cleaners.
Colored construction paper.
A ruler and crayons or colored pens.
White glue.

1. Cut light-colored (yellow is good) construction paper to fit the carton and paste it all around the four sides.

2. Take some darker colored paper and cut a piece 5½ in. by 3½ in. Paste it to the top of the carton to make the roof.

3. Measure carefully 6 in. up from the bottom of the carton on both front and back. Then measuring across the width of the carton, find the exact center (probably about 1⅜ in. from the edge) and make marks, front and back.

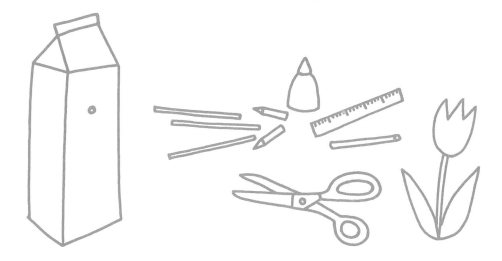

4. Make *sure* you have help from an older person on this step. Ask him or her to make holes in front and back at the places marked in step 3. The holes should be just big enough to fit the drinking straw through them snugly.

5. Cut the straw to a length of 4¼ in. and push it through both holes, leaving about ¾ in. sticking out in front.

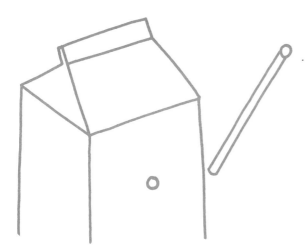

6. Twist two pipe cleaners together exactly at their middles to form a cross.

7. Take a third pipe cleaner and twist one end around the place where the others cross so that it sticks straight out from there . . . like this:

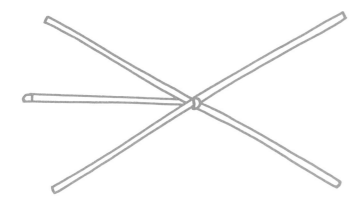

8. Then stick the long, straight cleaner through the straw from the front.

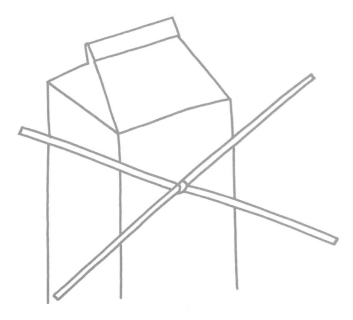

9. You now have the arms of your windmill; all you need are the sails.

10. Cut four pieces of paper to 2 in. by 1½ in. and fold them in half, lengthwise. Paste them around the ends of the arms, all heading in the same direction and all slanting away from the mill. These are the sails that catch the wind.

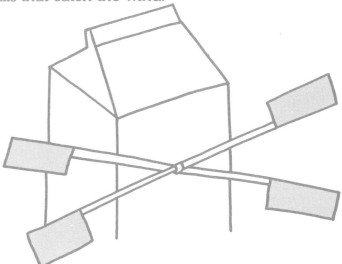

This is your windmill. You can turn the end of the pipe cleaner that sticks out the back to make the arms turn. Or perhaps you'll be able to turn them the way the wind would, by blowing on the sails.

To make your mill look more real, draw a door and some windows and maybe some Dutch tulips growing around the bottom.

Facing the Dutch Windmill Playtime

Windmills use the power of the wind to help people do heavy work. Before the electric motor and steam engine were invented, windmills pumped water and ground grain into flour. They are still used to pump water on farms where electricity is scarce. And more and more they are being used to produce electricity to help solve the energy problem.

Modern windmills look like this:

Long ago, there were many, many windmills, especially in the country we call Holland. Because these windmills were so beautiful, Dutch artists have always loved to paint pictures of them. When you go to the library, ask to see a book about Dutch painting. It will probably have some pictures of old Dutch windmills very much like the one you've made.

Here is a drawing of an old Dutch windmill. Color it in the way you think it should look. Then look in your library book to see how the Dutch artists used their colors.

COLOR-IN WINDMILL

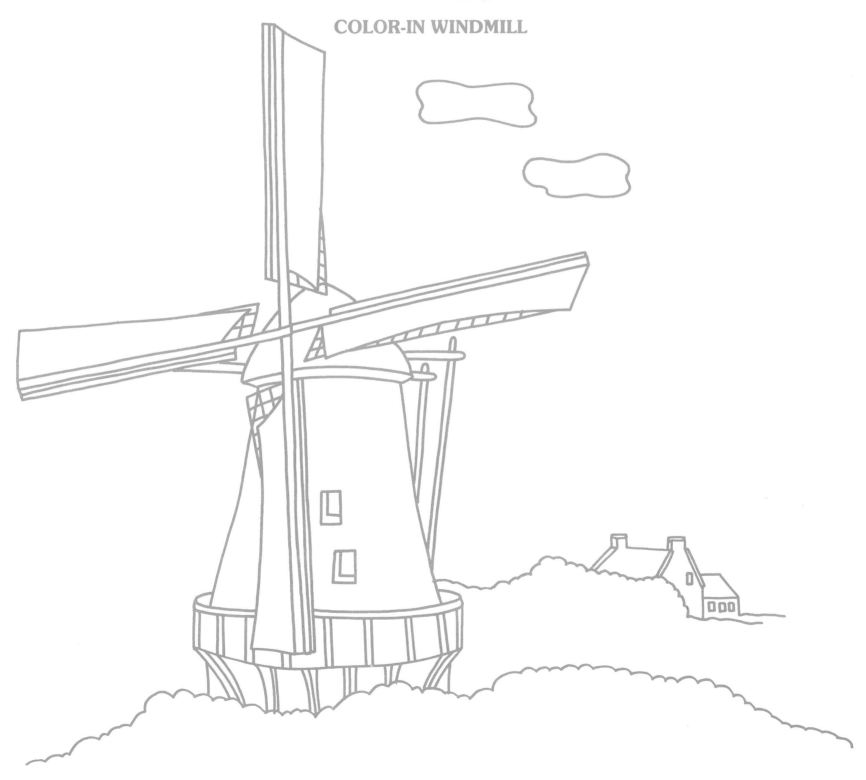

COLOR-IN MR. MOOSE AND BUNNY RABBIT

Did you know that two people can have exactly opposite feelings about one thing. It's true. We all see our world according to our own feelings, and often people have different feelings about the same event. Sometimes that leads to an argument. Take Phoebe and Homer, for example.

THE FALLINGS LEAVES

It was a windy October day. As Phoebe and Homer were walking home from school, bright orange and red leaves blew from the trees, swirled around in the air, and then fluttered gently to the ground.

"The leaves are really falling now," said Phoebe.

"I know," said Homer, "It makes you feel sad, doesn't it?"

"Sad? You mean happy, Homer. It makes you feel happy."

"No, Phoebe! It makes me feel *sad!*"

"Homer," said Phoebe, in a very annoyed tone, "it makes you feel *happy.* Because, Homer, when the leaves fall off the trees it means winter is coming—and that means we'll soon be able to go ice-skating and sledding."

"Phoebe," said Homer crossly, "when the leaves fall off the trees, it means summer is over—and that means no more swimming—and that is why we should be sad."

"Ha!" said Phoebe.

Just then there was a big gust of wind. The trees swayed and shivered and dropped more of their leaves.

"Hooray!" shouted Phoebe.

"Oh, no!" said Homer, sadly.

"Homer, if you liked ice-skating and sledding you wouldn't be saying, 'Oh, no'," Phoebe insisted.

"And if you liked swimming, you wouldn't be saying, 'Hooray'," answered Homer.

The two walked in silence for a while, each annoyed that the other could be so wrong about a simple thing and not be willing to admit it. Even the wind was still, as if to hear who would give in—but neither did. Then, impatient, the wind blew a great gust; and leaves came fluttering down making whispering sounds as they fell.

Phoebe jumped happily up and down. "Listen, Homer. It's almost as if they're saying, 'Winter is coming! Get your skates! Get your skates!' "

Homer tried once more to explain. "Leaves don't talk, Phoebe! But if they did they'd be saying sadly, 'Put away your snorkle and fins for the winter—it's all over until next year'."

"Ha!", snorted Phoebe.

Homer's face turned red. "Do you know that you go 'Ha!' whenever you can't think of something to say?"

"Ha!", said Phoebe.

Once more they walked along without speaking, but Homer was still puzzled. It was he who broke the silence. "Phoebe, how come I feel one way and you feel exactly the opposite about the very same thing?"

"That's simple, Homer," said Phoebe. "One of us is wrong."

But Homer wasn't so sure. "Does everybody have to feel the same way about everything?" he asked.

Suddenly Phoebe wasn't quite so sure. "W-e-l-l . . ." she said, thinking. "Well . . . I suppose if I liked swim-ming as much as you do, I'd be sad to see winter come, too."

"Thank you, Phoebe," said Homer, brightening. "I guess if I liked ice-skating and sledding as much as you, I'd be happy about the falling leaves."

"Thank you, Homer," said Phoebe softly.

They walked on. More leaves fluttered down in their path.

"The leaves are falling," said Phoebe.

"Yes," said Homer. "Isn't it sad?"

"Yes," said Phoebe. "Isn't it wonderful!"

"Yes," said Homer.

You see, both Homer and Phoebe were right—according to their own feelings. The next time you have a disagreement with a sister or brother or friend, stop and think about how the other person feels. Maybe—just maybe—you're both right.

Bob Colleary

The tiger is a member of the cat family

THE BENGAL TIGER

The Bengal tiger is a splendid beast.
He lives in Asia, south and east.
From the tip of his nose to the tip of his tail,
He's ten feet long—
And very strong.

The tiger is the only cat that likes to swim

The Bengal tiger prefers to eat nothing but meat.
So he's called a carnivore.
He wears the stripes his father wore
And his great grandfather wore before.

He loves the water when the jungle's hot,
And when it's hot, he drinks a lot.
He hasn't a shower, there are no pipes,
So he dips in a pool to cool his stripes.

The tiger walks so carefully
He hardly makes a sound,
When he puts his big paws on the ground.
With a stealthy pace and a steady grace
The tiger keeps moving and moving around . . .
The tiger keeps moving around.

Stan Davis

THE TOWN WITHOUT A DRAGON

Many long years ago, in a faraway kingdom, there lived a gallant and fearless knight whose name was Bold Sir Billingsworth. He travelled throughout the countryside seeking to do Good Deeds—and as he rode from town to town, the people would welcome him with cheers, for he was very famous, and much loved.

One day, Bold Sir Bill chanced upon a tiny town called Dragonburg, a lovely place with a big front gate. Standing before the gate was the leader of the town, the Kindly Count Curlycue. He was wringing his hands in worriment, so Sir Billingsworth jumped from his horse and said:

"Good and kindly Count, you seem worried—perhaps I can be of help!"

"Would that you could, Bold Knight," said the Count, "but I fear all is lost. You see, our problem is—the dragon!!"

"The dragon??" asked bold Sir Bill, amazed. "Gadzooks—have no fear! I will frighten the beast away!"

"But we don't *want* to frighten him away—we want our dragon back!" said Count Curlycue. "You see, once upon a time our little town was famous for its fierce and mighty dragon. People flocked from miles around to visit us and see our dragon, who lived right there in his dragon house. We were famous! We were proud!"

"But then one day, our mighty dragon left his dragon house and disappeared into the hills! We searched for him and found him, and we offered him many rewards if he would just come back to our town. But alas! He refused! And now no one ever comes to visit us anymore—because we're a town without a dragon! What misery, what shame!"

There are cities without sidewalks,
And counties without cats.
There are barns without barnyards,
And hamlets without hats.
I even know a belfry that doesn't have a bat,
But a town without a dragon is sadder, far, than that!
Yes, a town without a dragon is a town without a name.
And now that he has left us we will never be the same!
No self-respecting visitor will enter at our door
Till our town without a dragon—has its dragon back
    once more!!

Well, when the Bold Knight heard this terrible tale, he at once promised the kindly Count that he would go and speak to the dragon. So off he rode, up and down and around and around, until he reached the hilly cavern where the dragon was hiding. He jumped from his horse and shouted:

"Come out, fierce and mighty dragon! It is I—Sir Bill!"

"What do you want?" sniffed the dragon.

"Why, you're not so fierce and mighty at all," said Sir Bill. "In fact, I do believe you're *crying!* But why?"

"Because being a fierce and mighty dragon just isn't any fun! I mean, breathing fire and growling may appeal to some people—but I never wanted to be fierce and scary! I just wanted to be friendly! That was all, but nobody wanted to be *my* friend! Sure, they offered me great rewards to come back—but they don't really care about *me!* So now I've left, to live a lonely and forgotten dragon's life. And do you know why? I'll tell you why—because I've learned that:

Nobody loves a dragon,
Nobody wants to spend
Some time to play—or even say
'I like you; you're my friend'.

Everyone loves a flower,
Like a rose or a daffodil—
But nobdoy loves a dragon,
And nobody ever will!

"You know, if just one person in the whole town would really want to be my friend, I might come back but . . . it's no use."

Well, when Bold Sir Bill had heard the dragon's sad story, he jumped back on his horse and rode to town, where he told Kindly Count Curlycue of all he had seen and heard. To which the Count replied, "Friends with a dragon? Impossible! Why, it's never been done! Nobody loves a dragon!"

And so it seemed. But just then, there came a voice from behind the Count—the voice of his beautiful daughter, Lovely Lucinella:

"I do; I love the dragon! . . . Oh, he's not much to look at, I suppose—but for all his growling and fire-breathing, he's never said a mean thing to anybody! Yes, *I* want to be his friend!"

And as the lovely Lucinella spoke, a wondrous thing happened. Everyone in the town began to realize that they, too, loved the dragon—and everyone wanted to be his friend.

And kindly Count Curlycue said, "Thanks to my lovely daughter, we've seen the light! We must go tell the dragon right away!"

So off they rode, up and down and around and around to the dragon's cave in the hills.

"Dragon! Come out at once!" they called.

"What is it this time?" asked the dragon.

And then the people burst into cheers "Hooray for the dragon." And Kindly Count Curlycue read from a scroll:

"For service above and beyond the call of duty, and because we *all* love you, our Town awards you the special 'Best Friend' medal!"

"Golly," said the dragon.

"And now, will you come back to Dragonburg and live forever with your new friends?" asked the Count.

"I sure will! . . . Golly!" said the dragon, fighting back the tears.

And so the dragon came back to the town of Dragonburg. And once again the people were happy, because:

A town that has a dragon is a town that wears a smile!
And now that he's come back to us, we're smilin' all
    the while!
We've learned our lesson well and we
have found a brand-new friend,
And our town without a dragon
Has its dragon back . . .

The End!

Bob Brush

71

Here's a fun idea—paper -plate masks

PAPER PLATE MASKS

On the bottom of a paper plate draw any kind of funny face you like. Let's try Town Clown.

Then ask Mother or some other grown-up to cut out the eyes and mouth and make two small holes, one on each side. Tie pieces of string through these holes so that you can tie them around your head to hold on the mask.

Have someone cut out the eyes and mouth and all around the nose *except* at the top.

Cut a necktie like this one—about 1 foot long from a piece of gray or blue construction paper, and paste it in the proper place in the Captain's collar. Attach strings the same as for Town Clown and you can be your own Captain.

How about a Captain Kangaroo mask?

Use another paper plate and draw the Captain's face and collar on the bottom—something like this—

Make up some funny face masks. If you do this with your friends, you can make up little plays to act out in your mask disguises.

JOKE PAGE

Captain: What's the difference between an elephant and a peanut butter sandwich?

Mr. Moose: An elephant doesn't stick to the roof of your mouth.

Captain: Which is more important, the Sun or the Moon?

Mr. Moose: The Moon!

Captain: Why do you say that?

Mr. Moose: Because the Moon shines at night when it's dark, and the Sun shines during the day when it's light anyhow.

Captain: What goes zzub-zzub?

Mr. Moose: A bee flying backwards.

Captain: What goes oom-oom?

Mr. Moose: A cow walking backwards.

Captain: How did the firefly feel when he backed into the fan?

Mr. Moose: De-lighted!

Captain: What's the best way to catch a squirrel?

Mr. Moose: Go into the woods and act like a nut.

Captain: What's green and pecks on trees?

Mr. Moose: Woody Woodpickle.

Captain: How did the cow put her husband to sleep?

Mr. Moose: She made him a bulldozer.

Captain: What's grey, has four legs, a tail, and a trunk?

Mr. Moose: A mouse going on a trip.

IMPORTANT
or
Dooley O'Donahugh's Tuba

On the rocky coast of a northern sea, there once was a small fishing village. It didn't look very important—no large mansions or big town hall—but it was filled with important people.

One important person was Mrs. O'Donahugh. She was important because she ran the lighthouse that stood overlooking the sea. She kept it clean and bright, and made sure the light in the tower was always ready to guide the village's one fishing boat home through the dark nights and the thick fogs.

Then there were the sailors: MacDougal, Captain of the *Liza T. Magee*; and MacSweeny the helmsman, who steered a steady course; and MacGregor, who strung the fishing nets. Each morning they would put out to sea to catch the fish that fed the people of the village. And each evening, they would follow the beacon of the little lighthouse back to the safety of the village harbor. Their work was very important, and they loved their life on the sea.

Yes, everyone had an important job . . . well, almost everyone. One person who did not feel important was Mrs. O'Donahugh's son, Dooley.

You see, Dooley was best known in the village for his tuba playing. Of course he was still learning, but everyone knew that if he kept practicing—someday he would be a fine tuba player. The trouble was that Dooley didn't think tuba playing was IMPORTANT.

"I don't want to be a tuba player," he said to his mother. I want to do something IMPORTANT like . . . like running the lighthouse."

"Someday, perhaps—when you're older," said his mother. "Right now the most important thing for you is to practice your tuba." And off she went to polish the beacon in the lighthouse.

Dooley tried to practice—just to please his mother, but he had too many other things on his mind— IMPORTANT things. So before long, he put down his tuba and tiptoed down to the docks where the *Liza T. Magee* was getting ready to put out to sea.

"Hello, Captain MacDougal; hello, MacSweeny; hello, MacGregor," shouted Dooley. "I have good news for you. I have decided to be a sailor. I'm going to go to sea with you and climb the mast and spin the wheel and weave the nets."

"A fine idea," said MacSweeny. "We'd love to have you."

"That's right," said MacGregor. "But you're a bit young now, aren't ye, lad?"

"Aye," said the Captain. "Just be patient a few more years."

"But I want to do something IMPORTANT—now!" sobbed Dooley.

"And ye will someday," said MacSweeney. "Right now, the most important thing is to practice your tuba."

"That's the truth," said MacDougal. "You're the most important tuba player we have."

"And the loudest," laughed the Captain. "Cast off!" he shouted, and the *Liza T.* set sail leaving Dooley alone on the shore. He sat on a rock and watched through tear-filled eyes as the little boat disappeared below the horizon.

"That does it!" said Dooley to himself. "No one believes that I can do anything IMPORTANT . . . so I won't do anything at all. Most of all—I'll never play the tuba again!"

Dooley was so busy with his thoughts that when he heard his mother calling him, he was surprised to see that darkness was creeping over the harbor, and the sun was a fuzzy red ball sinking behind a great grey wall of fog that was rolling in from the sea.

"Dooley, Dooley," Mrs. O'Donahugh shouted. "The beacon in the lighthouse has gone out. The sailors won't be able to find their way home."

"Don't worry, Mother," said Dooley. "They'll follow the coastline. They know their way."

"Not in this fog," said Mr. O'Donahugh. "It's thicker 'n pea soup out there. They'll be lost for certain."

And sure enough, on the *Liza T.* Magee Captain Mac-Dougal could not see as far as the top of the mast. "It's no use," he said, "Not a sign of the lighthouse. If we don't see that beacon soon, we'll be washed up on the rocks and the boat will sink . . . and that's the truth."

Back on shore Dooley and his mother tried everything they could think of to fix the beacon; but nothing worked. Then, suddenly, Dooley had an idea . . . an IMPORTANT idea! He ran home and got his tuba.

"Dooley!" said Mrs. O'Donahugh in despair, "All the times I've asked you to practice . . . and you pick NOW when we must do something to help our fishermen. How can you be thinking of your tuba at such a time."

"It's all right, Mother," said Dooley. "I have a plan. I remember that Captain MacDougal said my tuba playing was loud. I may not be as IMPORTANT as a lighthouse keeper, but I sure do know how to play this tuba."

And play he did, harder and louder than ever before. The sound rose through the fog and across the harbor; and when it reached the sea, it kept on floating over the waves.

On the *Liza T.*, the fog was thicker than ever, and the crew searched in vain for the lighthouse, but all was dark and still.

Then . . .

"What was that sound?" said MacSweeny. "Strangest seagull I've ever heard."

"That's no seagull", said Captain MacDougal. "That's Dooley's tuba! And it's comin' from that direction! Head for it, MacSweeny. We'll follow the sound to shore. Dooley will play us home!"

And so it was. Straight and true they sailed back to the safety of the harbor. And there was great happiness in the little village, for Dooley had truly saved the *Liza T. Magee* and her crew!

"Son, you've proven yourself tonight," said Mrs. O'Donahugh. "From now on you can help me tend the lighthouse."

"Yes," said Captain MacDougal, "and you can come fishin' with us any time."

"Thank you, all," said Dooley, "but I don't want to be a lighthouse keeper or a fisherman or a sailor anymore . . . I want to be a tuba player."

"Oh, do ye, now," said the Captain, "and why is that?"

"Why, because," said Dooley, "because it's IMPORTANT."

And so it was that young Dooley O'Donahugh found out how important he really was. And every single evening from that time on, when the sailors headed for home, they could hear the sound of Dooley's IMPORTANT TUBA, singing loud, and clear, and proud!

Bob Colleary

Here are some projects for those days when you have to stay in bed but don't really feel too sick.

STAY IN BED ACTIVITIES

Lapboard

It's a good idea to make this lapboard now, while you are well, so that you can use it if you get sick. Ask a grown-up for help with this one.

Get a strong cardboard box about 24 inches wide and at least 8 inches deep—ask at the supermarket for one of the cartons that large cans come in.

Leave the flaps on the ends of the box, but cut off the side flaps. Draw a large semi-circle on each of the long sides of the box and ask a grown-up to help you cut out those places where your legs will fit.

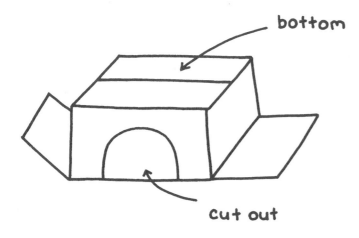

bottom

cut out

Tape the side flaps up on the outside, leaving a wedge-shaped space between them and the box.

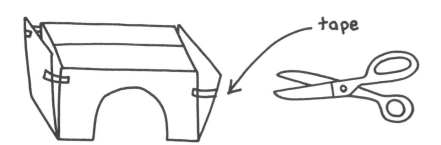

tape

If there is a ridge across the bottom of the box, cut a piece of cardboard to fit the bottom and paste it to the box. This is your working or writing surface.

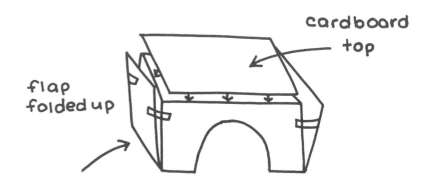

cardboard top

flap folded up

Now you have a good place to draw or write or work on projects when you have to stay in bed.

There are many things on other pages of this book that you can do in bed, but here are some more good projects.

Jigsaw Puzzles

Draw a picture on a piece of shirt cardboard, then color it in. With a ruler draw a number of lines across the picture in different directions. Cut along the lines and you have made your own jigsaw puzzle.

Or you can paste a picture from a magazine onto cardboard and cut it the same way. Make as many different puzzles as you want, but remember to keep them in separate boxes or envelopes so that the pieces won't get mixed up. Turn the page! There's a puzzle for you to cut out and color in.

Hand and Finger Drawing

Place your hand on a blank piece of paper, trace around it with a pencil, then see what kind of picture you can make from the outline. Try putting your hand in different positions, and using parts of your hand and fingers to add to the shape. Finally draw in details like eyes, ears, mouth, nose, scales, tails, or whatever is needed to finish the figure.

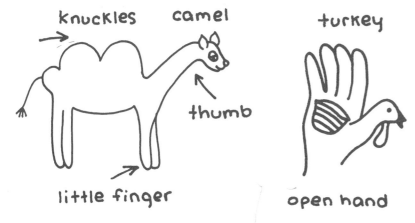

See how many different animals and other figures you can make.

Wall Shadows

Here's another way to put your hands to work making pictures. You'll need a strong light (the room should not be too bright), and a blank wall or big piece of cardboard on which to make shadows. Hold your hand or hands between the light and your "screen" to make a dark, sharp-edged shadow. Hold your hand in different positions to form shadow animals, birds, fish, and even people.

Keep experimenting. There are many shadow shapes that you will be able to make.

Real-Life Pictures

Try drawing (using your lapboard for a desk) pictures of the objects in your room: a lamp, some flowers, the window, a toy, a chair. Look at your "model" often and try to make your drawing as close to the real thing as you can.

77

79

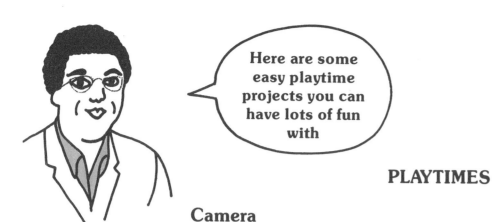

Here are some easy playtime projects you can have lots of fun with

PLAYTIMES

Camera

For your make-believe camera you'll need a small cardboard box—about half the size of a shoebox . . . or an empty facial tissue box will do.

Color or paint the box black . . . or cover it with black construction paper. If the box has a lid make sure it is taped on tightly.

Next, ask an older person to cut a paper cup in half—like this—

If you can't find a paper cup, make a tube of white construction paper like this—

then tape the top part of the cup—or the paper tube to the front of your box.

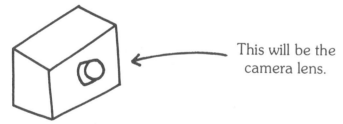

This will be the camera lens.

Next, take a cardboard toilet paper tube and tape it to the top of the box.

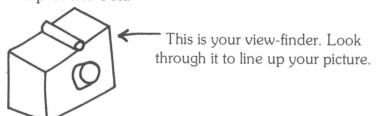

This is your view-finder. Look through it to line up your picture.

Finally, take the plastic cap from an empty toothpaste tube and paste it to the top of the box—like this—

This is the button you push to take a picture.

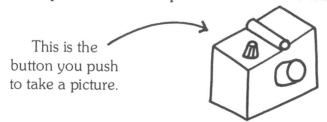

Now you have a playtime camera. You can pretend to take pictures of your family and friends. Just look through the view-finder, say "Hold it!" or "cheese" and push the button!

Binoculars

Binoculars are powerful glasses that make distant objects appear to be close

Here's how to make a "pretend" pair:
Tape two toilet paper tubes together, side by side.

tape

Have someone make a small hole in each tube—like this—

Tie the ends of a two-foot piece of heavy string through the holes:

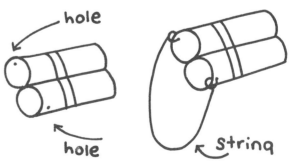

hole

hole

string

Slip the string loop over your head and let your binoculars hang down at your chest.

When you hold them up to your eyes and look through them, you can be a ship's captain, or a bird watcher, or a racehorse owner watching your horse win the Kentucky Derby.

JOKE PAGE

Captain: What does your watch say?
Mr. Moose: Nothing, silly, watches can't talk.

Captain: If I take five apples from ten apples, what's the difference?
Mr. Moose: That's what I say, what's the difference.

Captain: If you put ten ducks in a carton, what would you have?
Mr. Moose: A box of quackers.

FABLES

Long, long ago, in Greece there lived a storyteller named Aesop. Aesop's stories are called fables. They are often about animals who act like people. Each fable teaches a lesson about the wisdom, or foolishness, or pride, or greed of humans. The lesson of a fable is called its "moral".

Here are three of Aesop's fables. See if you can figure out the lesson that each one teaches. Then check the morals, printed upside down at the bottom of the page, to see if you were right.

The Wind and the Sun

An argument arose between the north wind and the sun as to which of them was the more powerful. To settle the dispute, they decided to see which would be able to get the cloak from off the back of a traveller on the road beneath them.

The north wind started the contest with strong, strong, icy blasts to try and blow the cloak away. But the harder the wind blew, the tighter the man wrapped his cloak around him.

The sun laughed at the wind's failure and turning in the direction of the traveller, smiled warmly upon him. The more the sun smiled, the warmer the man became until he took off his cloak and sat in the shade of some trees by the side of the road.

The Boy and the Wolf

A shepherd boy, who tended his flock near a village, often amused himself by crying, "Wolf! wolf!" when there was no wolf in sight, so that he might laugh at the people who ran to help him. The trick succeeded several times until, one day, a wolf did come near the flock and the boy cried, "Wolf! wolf!" in earnest.

The villagers, supposing the boy to be up to his tricks again, paid no attention to his cries, and the wolf carried off one of his sheep.

The Fox and the Crow

A crow snatched a piece of cheese from a windowsill and flew with it to a tree.

A fox spied the crow with the delicious morsel and went and stood beneath the tree.

"Oh crow," he said, "what beautiful wings you have, and bright eyes. What a graceful neck is yours, and how handsome are your shiny feathers. Surely your voice must be as beautiful as you. Pray, sing for me that I may hear for myself."

The crow, pleased with the fox's flattery, opened his mouth to give a caw . . . and the cheese fell to the ground where the fox snapped it up and ate it.

"I may have praised your beauty," said the fox, "but I will not comment on your brains."

Morals

3. Beware of flatterers.

2. People that tell lies are not to be believed—even when they speak the truth.

1. Persuasion is better than force.

THE LIBRARY

There's a place—near where you live—that holds more adventures than you could ever imagine:

A trip to the moon—
A cave exploration—
A brand new baby—
A shipwreck—
The story of a lost kitten—
A volcano . . . A sparrow and a prince
Two boys on a raft . . . the circus—
The caterpillar and the butterfly—
—and thousands of other stories.

Do you know the place? It's the library.

There are as many adventures in the library as there are in the real world!

Have you been to the library? If not, ask Mom or Dad to take you there. What do you think you will see?

Books! That's right. Hundreds and hundreds of books!

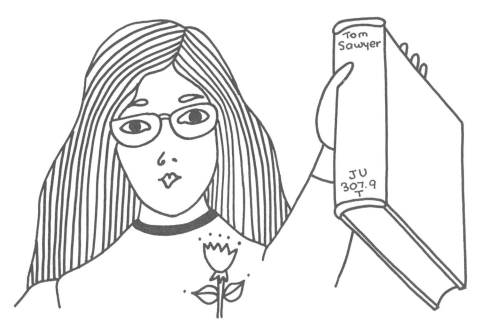

When you first go to the library, it will seem very big, and you won't know which books to pick. But there is someone who is there just to help you—the librarian. All you have to do is ask.

Later, when you get to know the library you will be able to find books by the numbers that the librarian gives to them.

Then you'll be able to find any book you want. Meanwhile, ask Mom or Dad . . . or the librarian, who will be glad to help you. Try asking about some of the things you've learned in this book: windmills, trains, rocks, leaves . . . or anything you want to know about. It's all there in the library. And it's all free!

THE HONEY BEE

The honey bee rarely stings.
She's much too busy with other things.
The buzzing you hear is the sound of her wings
As, hour after busy hour,
She sips from flower after flower.

Back at the hive, the place is alive
With workers waiting on their queen
And putting nectar into cells
To turn to honey when it jells . . .
A very, very busy scene.

But the Queen is quiet and serene.
She stays at home
With honey comb.
You can't expect her
To gather nectar.
That's the job of the little blob
Who works for free . . .
The honey bee.

© Saugatuck Productions

BALLAD OF THE GRAY WHALE

With a powerful thrust of her great tail,
The gray whale moves through the sea.
Thousands of miles to the south she'll go
To the blue green waters of Mexico.

She's a mammal like a camel
Or a dog or a cat
Or you or me.
It just happens that
She lives in the sea.
She's as big as a bus
And weighs a lot more
Her tail is as broad as a big barn door.
Say that she looks different if you wish
But she's certainly not—a fish.

Stan Davis

© Halrone Music
Reprinted by special permission.

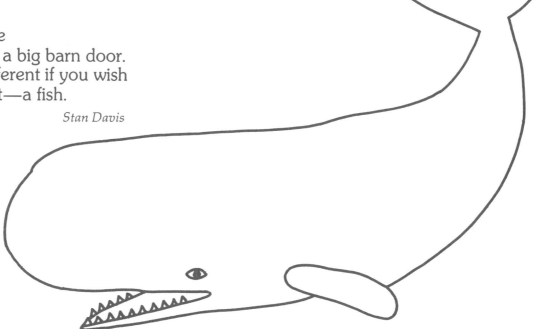

You humans have really funny paws. Here's a poem about them.

FEET

Got somethin' to tell you and I think it's really neat
At the lowest end of the human body
Are the feet.
You will see them on the road
On the sand
And 'way down town on the street.
Have you ever noticed the kind of shoes
That people choose to wear?
The kind of shoes that people choose
Usually come by the pair:
You get black shoes, red shoes, short shoes, tall.
Some people wear no shoes at all!

There are several ways you can use your feet:
You can walk
You can run
You can dance to a beat
And you can stand right there
On the sand right there and
Dig your little toes in the sand if you care.

In the human foot there are twenty-six bones
Twenty-six bones right next to the ground
That's a lot of bones to be movin' around!

Stan Davis

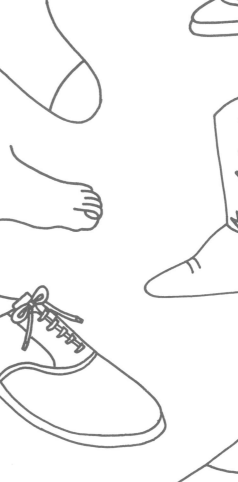

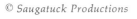

Dot·to·Dot
Follow the dots in order.

THE APPLES AND THE KING

by Frank Abatemarco

Once upon a time, long, long ago there lived a good and wise king who was loved by all his subjects. In fact, this king had only one weakness: he loved apple pie. But, alas, there were no apple trees in his kingdom. The nearest apples were in a distant land on the other side of the forest. So, once a month, the king would send his messenger through the forest to get some apples for his pie.

It was a long hard journey of two days and two nights, and the king would wait impatiently until the tired messenger would return with two of the biggest, finest apples he could find. The king would be pleased, but, alas, it took four apples to make a pie and the messenger could carry only two at a time—one in each hand. So the poor fellow would have to set out again on the long, hard journey through the forest.

When at last the exhausted messenger would stumble home with two more apples, the king would be very happy, for now he could have his pie. And the messenger would be happy because finally he could get some rest . . . until the next month.

And so it went for years, until one day, when the king bade the messenger go to the other side of the forest for the second pair of apples, the fellow just smiled and said, "Not this time, Your Majesty."

The king was flabbergasted! "What?" he shouted. "You know that four apples are required to make a pie and you have brought me only two. Do you dare to disobey your king?!"

But the messenger only smiled a broader smile as he took two more apples from his coat and gave them to the king.

"How did you do that?" cried the king. "It's some kind of trick!"

Then the messenger showed the king two pockets that had been sewn in his coat by a wonderful tailor in the kingdom beyond the forest. The king marvelled at them, for he had never seen pockets before.

Now the king was extremely happy, he would no longer have to wait so long to get enough apples for an apple pie. The messenger was happy too—he wouldn't have to do all that extra running back and forth through the forest.

So the very next day the king had his own tailor sew pockets on his royal cloak and ordered him to sew on pockets for all the people of his kingdom. And from that day on, everyone in the kingdom was a little bit happier.

THE DAY THE COLORS WENT AWAY

Jennifer Sweet is not very neat.
She isn't the tidiest person you'll meet.
She loves to paint pictures but so in a rush
She never takes care of her paints or her brush.
She doesn't use water to keep her brush clean
And mixes the yellow with blue, red and green.
The poor little colors, then try though they may
Get mixed all together and wind up as gray.

Jennifer's angry, and starts to complain.
She tears off the paper, and starts in again.
And everything soon is a terrible mess
With paint on her face, and paint on her dress.
"That does it!" said Jennifer, "Finished! I'm through.
I can't paint a picture whatever I do.
There's paint on my face, and it's smeared anyway."
And she threw down her brush, and she ran off to
play.

Up jumped the paints in a terrible huff.
"We don't have to put up with that . . . that's
enough!"
They called all the colors and whirled them about
And all of the colors just followed them out.
They whisked through the garden as fast as can be,
And took all the green from each leaf and each tree.
The flowers' bright colors and blue of the sky
All vanished, alas, without saying goodbye.

Then back in came Jennifer, hearing a noise
She stared at her room, and her dress and her toys.
"Oh where have the colors gone? . . . what did they
   do?"
But deep down inside, little Jennifer knew.
She picked up the paintbox and hurried away
Out into the garden so gloomy and gray.
She stared at the flowers, the trees, and the sky.
She felt so unhappy, she wanted to cry.

Oh it's terribly sad
When the colors you had
Simply vanish away
And you're left with just gray.
It's hard to be cheery
When everything's dreary
And the sky isn't blue
And it's all 'cause of you.

Oh what a shame, what an unhappy day
When all of the colors just vanished away.
Jennifer knew it was up to her now
To find them and bring them back safely somehow.
She followed a path till it finally led
To a great shining rainbow directly ahead.
And there were the colors all having such fun,
"I'll climb up and catch them all, every last one."

She first caught the green one and then caught the red.
"I'll treat them all gently . . . I promise," she said.
Then yellow and purple and blue . . . ah at last
All safe in the box, as she shut the lid fast.
"I'll take better care of them, now that I see
How sad little paints when they're messy can be."
And hurrying back, one last promise she gave . . .
"I'll try to be careful . . . and try to behave."

Jennifer brought the colors she caught
Back home to the garden to clean them, she thought.
But out came the lizard and asked if she would
Please paint back his colors and make him look good.
Then up the poor colorless butterfly flew
And said, "Please, dear Jennifer, please paint me, too."
The flowers all crowded around in a rush
For pretty red paint from our Jennifer's brush.

"Goodness," said Jennifer, "What shall I do?"
My heavens, there just are too many of you."
She went to the paints and she said, "I'll be good . . .
If you give back their colors . . . if only you would."
Then wonder of wonders . . . as quick as you please
The colors returned to the grass and the trees
And everything soon had a wonderful hue . . .
The flowers, the sky, and our Jennifer too!

Jennifer Sweet, I'm bound to repeat
Was never the tidiest person you'd meet.
But Jennifer's different since Jennifer learned
This lesson when all of the colors returned:
That paints are like people, and so they expect
That they will be treated with love and respect.
And if you take care of them properly, they . . .
Will make your world bright as a rainbow each day.

Susan Birkenhead

COLOR-IN JENNIFER'S GARDEN

Here's what Jennifer's garden looked like when all the colors were gone. With your crayons, pens or paints, put the colors back the way *you* would like to see them.